COLL

NON-FICTION

*The Self on the Page: Theory and Practice of Creative
Writing in Personal Development* (with Celia Hunt)
The Healing Word
Creative Writing in Health and Social Care (editor)
A Fine Line: New Poetry from Eastern and Central Europe
(with Jean Boase-Beier and Alexandra Buchler)
Writing: Self and Reflexivity (with Celia Hunt)
On Listening
A Century of Poetry Review (editor)
Poetry Writing: the Expert Guide
Music Lessons: Newcastle Bloodaxe Poetry Lectures
Percy Bysshe Shelley (editor)
Beyond the Lyric: A Map of Contemporary British Poetry

POETRY

Folding the Real
The Distance Between Us
Common Prayer
Rough Music

TRANSLATOR

Evening Brings Everything Back (translations of Jaan Kaplinski)
Day (translations of Amir Or)

COLESHILL

Fiona Sampson

Chatto & Windus
LONDON

Published by Chatto & Windus 2013

2 4 6 8 10 9 7 5 3 1

Copyright © Fiona Sampson 2013

Fiona Sampson has asserted her right under the Copyright, Designs
and Patents Act 1988 to be identified as the author of this work

First published in Great Britain in 2013 by
Chatto & Windus
Random House, 20 Vauxhall Bridge Road,
London SW1V 2SA
www.randomhouse.co.uk

Addresses for companies within The Random House Group Limited can be found at:
www.randomhouse.co.uk/offices.htm

The Random House Group Limited Reg. No. 954009

A CIP catalogue record for this book
is available from the British Library

ISBN 9780701186470

The Random House Group Limited supports the Forest Stewardship Council® (FSC®),
the leading international forest-certification organisation. Our books carrying the FSC label
are printed on FSC®-certified paper. FSC is the only forest-certification scheme supported
by the leading environmental organisations, including Greenpeace. Our paper procurement
policy can be found at www.randomhouse.co.uk/environment

Printed and bound by CPI Group (UK) Ltd, Croydon CR0 4YY

Set in Bembo 12/14pt
Typeset by Palimpsest Book Production Limited, Falkirk, Stirlingshire

For my good neighbours

ACKNOWLEDGEMENTS

Some of these poems have appeared in *Artemis*, *New Humanist*, *New Statesman*, *Oxford Poetry*, *Poetry* (Chicago), *Poetry Ireland*, *Poetry London*, *PN Review*, *Spectator*, *Temenos*, *Yellow Nib* and *Alhambra Calendar* and, in translation, in *Literatur ir Menas* (Vilnius), *Poetiki* (Athens), and *Poljupci I Molitva* (selected poems), Edition Bronko Miljokovic (Nis). Some were commissioned by Genome Research Limited for the Wellcome Trust Sanger Institute; by Oxford Brookes University; and by the City of London Festival/Poet in the City. I am grateful for an Arts Council of England Grant for the Arts which enabled work on this book, and also for fellowships at the EKEMEL Literature House at Paros and at the Institute of English Studies, School of Advanced Study, University of London. I would like to thank Tim Liardet for his close-reading, and Parisa Ebrahimi for her editorial work.

CONTENTS

Dans une terre grasse et pleine d'escargots
Je veux creuser moi-même une fosse profonde

– Charles Baudelaire, 'Le Mort joyeux'

PRELUDE

November
makes blue smudges
between trees,
sfumato —

drifts down the lane
familiar
as the neighbour
I call fear.

Again this occlusion,
this instability
of light.
Again the unseen thumb

printing the lens
as I lift it shining
to my eye.

CANTO

I'm suspended. Below me
is a dark pool.
When I plunge a hand in,
water breaks on my palm —
a splash
      of black mercury.

All of us, floating and stalking,
are flat-footed insects, water-boatmen
dimpling the dark.

LITTLE VIRGILS

Night after night the guides come,
old enemies, old rivals
      and A— as he was

ten years ago.
They pass close,
      speaking in their new

night voices
and they see me,
      oh, they see me –

Laughing, shaking,
crying, I'm as real to them
      as one of those on-screen heroines,

huge, bright-skinned,
her eyes filling
      with the world's tears –

SONNET ONE – A DREAM

These warm spring nights, it seems as if
you float in formless dark;
your dreaming mind seems somehow close
to limitless
and all the world at stake.

. . . Something in the room shifts
and wakes you. Like lace dropping
lightly on your face,
a draught enters your dream
and lifts it from its tracks.

The incubus is back; he's on your chest,
half absence, half beast
grown fat on lack.
He settles in to break you: break the dream.

ORPHIC

The vixen was a silhouette.
In milk, perhaps in whelp,
she trod and trod.
Her mistake was forming
like shadow in the muscle.

At night each thing
smells sweet
and full of signals,
the verge-plants are coarsely drawn
with ink.

       Propped akimbo
the soiled fox seems to mouth
some vast affront,
her head thrown back all jaw
a long bone

made to resonate –
a cleated bone
made to string then pluck –
the way a wheel is strung
from its rim.

FROM THE ADULTERER'S SONGBOOK

Return at night.
What remains
is one
clear note,

the night odour
of living air
almost-descant,
almost out

of reach, like roses'
fugitive aroma,
that last note held –

SONNET TWO – THE DEATH THREAT

The early dark thrums with wings,
shadows scud between headlights.
A window at the road's end gleams
like a gaze: too long, misplaced.

He changes shape. The autumn nights
permit this, with their mint of smells,
the ash-and-damp notes of a dream
you remember, blurred as wings

flurrying into a windscreen:
huge eyes, blackened by the lights,
because sometimes he's an owl. Or he's a swan,
or *Caucasian male, clean-shaven, age unknown* –

or this plumed and gleaming angel
at the door, with a knife.

THE CHANGES

Grandsire Doubles – 25 Feb 1939; Doubles (9 methods) – 5 June 1991;
Surprise Minor (7 methods) – 4 Nov 2002; Spliced Minor (14 methods) –
20 Feb 2011

— Felstead Database of Peals, *Coleshill Tower*

Water is plasma
shuddering in combination,
the grass shudders,
the bluebells
are a shuddering haze

and your blood is honey.
It stays in the mouth
like guilt,
rumour, grief,
a necessary meal.

I'm afraid
of the untouched body,
silence,
the priest waiting
in the garden.

*

Your blood is honey.
It fills the mouth
like guilt,
rumour, grief.
A necessary meal,

but what's nearer
or more real
than the sweetness
in the vein,
that sticky dew?

Will the freshet
in the cup
rinse away the taste
of lamb and salt,
oil and rosemary?

*

Elected silence
stirs
as if to say
Before you were, I am.
Local, huge,

it's full
of the milkiness of wings,
rain-light,
the sussuration
of hungers.

Your blood is honey,
stays in the mouth
like guilt,
shame, grief,
those necessary meals.

*

Once again
the prayer room

with its milky light,
its private,
pragmatic silence.

Your blood is honey.
It stays in the mouth
like guilt,
rumour, grief:
their sweet and salt

is to be eaten
here, among red armchairs,
in the odour
of new carpet;
to be eaten now.

*

Is it right —
to be the lamb
who must trust the shepherd,
which is to say death?
Your blood is honey.

The priest smokes a cigarette
among the shadows
in the silent garden,
Lives of the Saints
under his arm.

Guilt, rumour,
grief —
look how they break
from the vein
into the surgeon's cup.

SONNET THREE – THE NIGHT-DRIVE

On the Buscot road

Driving at night, you catch yourself
feeling excited. Thick blossom
hangs, hallucinatory
in darkness, beside the road.

Half-way home. The miles slide,
tree after tree after tree after –
their blue flicker, like a dream
that brings you back to yourself

then lets you slip away again.
The dashboard clock floats up through glass,
its limbic digits in blue reverse.

Things seem to swell and stall –
blooming into close-up – then the tall
trees and the grass glide past again.

EMILY AMONG THE ASTRONOMERS

There is at Coleshill a limestone spur known as Kings Hill, a site
much used by the astronomers of that district.
                                        – Berkshire Antiquities

We build—star-ward—
But something—makes us fall.
Nor warehouses—nor yards
Conserve us all

But self-enclosed—
Like Emily—we stare
And yearn—though skies disclose
No pilot star—

Till in the black
We nudge—a new landfall—
And each gaze bounces back
Its sweet—unstable—all.

SONGS FOR POLL'S BEES

Swarm

Very deep,
very mobile
the swarm-song
sounds in my chest:
not a beat, not breath

but an older music
remembered –
as a head
turns on a pillow
or hips lift –

one gesture becoming another
in the room
when a shoulder moves
close, then moves away
uncovering a picture-window

filled with blossom-streaks,
pale trailers
that might be rain
or jet-trails –
but these are flowers

swarming white and eager
on dark branches,
while the Airbus
overhead
shakes the glass.

Bee-song

The song rises from long grass
to make a mouth between the trees,
rising and opening
as if it will never be done:

opens its dark mouth
breathing and rising,
sound filling the space of sound
mostly secret most necessary

trembling and calling
itself out of the dark
ceaselessness of itself,
unendingly re-forming

dark in the darkened clearing
between the maize headlands and the trees
with the evening gathering
in the long grass –

Bee Samā'

If God were limitless geometry –
the perfection world
reaches clumsily over itself
to articulate:
If he could be glimpsed in the pattern
of limitless addition –
but were not that pattern, beautiful
though the turquoises
and greens of the glazed tiles are,
so beautiful
that the eye swoons, dropping through
endless form: If God
were neither principle nor dream – resting
his cheek on the earth
for a moment you might have imagined,
a gift of pure grace
from a Perfection that is bodiless
here and everywhere:
Bees could be his servants and prophets,
demonstrating beauty
is a kind of humility –
as tonight they offer
no more than the hive's aroma.

The Karst in August

Bee-boards bleach
in the couch grass
on high fields.
               No-one goes there,
no-one takes the steep goat tracks
past ruined farms.

I remember the secret you told me,
and how the abandoned hulls
turn nailed flanks to the sun
and sink
         in a murmur of bees,
bees flecking the air brightly –

their hum is a rumour,
an old tune.

Winter Bees

Every year
the weak January sun
brings bumblebees
nudging and thudding against the wood
of my work shed –
which must give out some old pine sweetness
soft in the grain
under the blue cracked paint, a blue
miracle sky.
Banal, but it moves us –
a small spring
resurrection, in the time
just before spring.

What tender precision
directs each bee
to this recurring conversation,
its compass set
by the sun's contracted arc?
The bee Christ
wears his gilded crown of mourning
for the station
of the winter swarm.
Out of strength
came forth sweetness. Our dark
hearts are hives.

SONNET FOUR – CONCEPTION

The small cat inside the hut,
looking out of the door's glass
at the dog scratching that door,
places her paws together
with unconscious care
on the blue square of the mat.

Grace is a secret clockwork,
she seems to say. Which is true –
we'll never arrive at that truth.
I mean, we can never undress
right down to how we were
in our conception's new caress

when the membrane spilled the dreaming yolk;
when self first broke and entered self.

THE CORN VERSICLES

securus judicat orbis terrarum
                    — St. Augustine

I love paths cut
        through corn,
through grass and meadowsweet —

        that clean opening,
as if the path
        were a pattern

for life,
        abstract and true —
as if form were a truth

        about you.
And I love to walk
        the new

swathe, where stalks
        start up from the exact
gold dark

        as I reach
down to touch each corn-head
        with a fingertip —

it makes me think
        of Helena, Empress
Mother of Constantine,

                    gambling on the natural justice
that gods
              reward faithfulness.

Everything good
              still waits
in the next field,

                    the best
is yet to come
                    and it smells of warm earth

crazed by sun,
              of seed-heads
husked against my thumb.

Do you remember
              when we
walked at Eastleach?

                    Did you see
me stoop and grow
              strange to myself –

like the rows
              of wheat – like shaking bells of husk?

A curtain brims;
its white lip appears,
dashing and slovenly
like the girl on the Tube
with her bedroom hair.

I miss that girl
crossing the Green
in heels and feather trim,
whom I so nearly
and never was.
                    Oh, waking
is a rising to light,
something humming
deep and dirty
moves through a suspended life,
in the dawning bedroom

the jacket on a chair-back
is a gesture
                suddenly stilled:
and the girl crossing the Green
turns her head on a pillow
barred with light.

SONNET FIVE – COLESHILL RESURRECTION

This dream starts in the middle.
Or a memory starts with this

like coming into childhood consciousness,
suddenly realising *I exist,*

waking from eternity . . .
dreamy, floating consciousness!

The clues are too vague
to make a neat Freudian riddle,

but you know you were driving
a road that showed now dark, now bright: film's

unstable light. Your fear grew – and grew –
and suddenly arrival

burst its white bouquet of flame
against the windscreen
                        you rose up to and through.

IMPETIGO MADRIGAL

In the sweet growing season
something bubbles up in me.
It bursts out as blisters,
and rain-clouds fill my palm.

Sometimes skin
weeps, when you can't bear to;
sometimes grief sweeps down
like April rain.

HYMN OF THE COLESHILL ORCHARDS

Mirabelles
and greengages
hang like lollies
in the trees'

four thousand lobes,
and wasps hang swooning
from the lobes
of fruit.

Your hand shifts here now here
among twigs, ripe fruit
and the corona
of insects.

What the wasps spoil
is sweetest;
they sow the ripeness
in the plum.

SONNET SIX – BY ASHEN COPSE

Follow the path
down through buttery mud
past flowering elder and hazel –
the dogs running ahead –

till the last farm
slips behind the trees
and you're alone
with a kind of wild fecklessness.

Sunshine, rain
and once again the crowsfoot
and lady's smock near the lane:

how these recur – a song
that some drunk you thought was done
starts up again.

I WAS GLAD WHEN THEY SAID UNTO ME

*Badbury Clumps is said to be the site of the Siege of Mons Badonicus,
and Arthur's twelfth consecutive victory against the Anglo-Saxons.*

In the midday rain
birds call from the covert
They improvise

cry after cry
out of the cross-hatched
wet dark

in a time of floods,
as rivers carry trout
leaping through the streets,

their flanks like water's muscle –
flexure, knot –
Rain streams down the windows

here below King Arthur's hill
making panes of water-glass;
stories thicken like floods

*

The bird takes the buckshot
a little way
in the up-loop

of her startled flight –
a bird now starred
with bloody flowers

carrying the air
or carried by air
through the green

and pale
designs of fields
Flight is

a gasp and rise
out of barley,
out of the yawing

wind-stirred corn
We're caught by this
sweet flurry

into time,
the shadow passing
through the barley

like a word
to race away
to disappear

at the daisied headland where
another bird is climbing

Purple fireweed
burns in the verge
all down the lane,
a parish of sun
and shade.

A crozier holds the glow
from lights strung high
in the chancel roof.
*Christ, what is the use
of all this grief?*

A GAME OF CARDS

Light seeps round the curtain
of my hotel room –
headboard, tapestry cushions,
a whispering gloss
that flatters the guests.
The light says,
                Just outside,

just after breakfast,
a glorious elsewhere is opening . . .
This is a poem
about windows – and doors –
that open and open
on another story
                just beyond

the velour and gilt-braid drapes.
It's such a shame to be singular –
who wouldn't steal
a bit more life,
nip and tuck?
Like the gap
                in the wheat

where a hare bounds out,
or the track that leads off
beyond the sidings,
possibility
loosens the shape of things . . .
What's through the square window today?
                        they asked

when we were small, and the world
unexhausted. And I saw
the den on the building site,
blackberry hedges,
a cricket on my thumb
and sun dazzling through grass.
                              Time went still, then,

as if the sunlight outsmarted it,
as it did at a gate in Vrsac,
where you grasped the wrought iron
and leaned into the camera
smiling –
in the album you're still smiling,
                              still undiagnosed –

Grace is not remission, could never be:
circumstance is so pitiless
parading its *The world is all that is the case.*
Sometimes what opens
is really closing, like Poznán's Old Market Square,
cobbles and arcades,
                    where they speak tourist German

because of what happened
in the squeezebox of history:
compress – release –
we should understand this,
our own lungs work air
that thickens
                because we grieve.

An opening's some kind of hopeful dream.
Paths, for example,
offer variations in light

like clues to where they're going.
And dream's an opening
into the brilliant world

              beyond the bedroom —

Even in this cushiony bed,
even to sunshine
and the smell of expensive Colombian coffee,
what disappointment
it is to wake
from a dream
         of difference.

SONNET SEVEN – THE REVENANT

Downhill . . . and I met myself,
a pale ghost glimmering
the way a poacher's torch shines
there – now there – between the trees

so it seems at moments as if
they too are ghosts, walking
in a new light, coming
out of memory towards you . . .

When we met, myself and I,
each cast the other into a kind
of shining shadow,

my younger self ascending through me
like a shiver, as I turned
toward the house below.

The magpie hangs by her feet.
Her eye could turn you to stone
if it ever opened.

DREAMSONGS

To dream of a house is always to dream of the body.

A blur of branches
Smells –
linden and dust,
diesel, frost –

You're running between ghost-trees
toward a house
that keeps growing
from the shadows

Dusk flows in
at your heels

Breaths like sighs
fill the dark,
shadows shift
room after dusty room

Somewhere
too close for comfort
a marble rolls
along the floorboards,

drrrrr drrrrr drrrrr
dink dink dink dink
                    dink

Now you're
climbing a staircase –
dim symmetry
If only form

were language,
if only these dim shapes
would form that word
you can't remember

Out of reach,
but it stirs the hairs
on your nape

LITTLE SONGS OF MALEDICTION 2

Imagine bees falling from the sky –
yes, all of them.
Small scabs of air.

SONNET EIGHT – SUMMER DUSK

On summer evenings
air thickens – and settles,
dust dropping onto shelves of books
silently – settles.
These evenings
lift from the pages of books,
or out of dreams.

Write your name in the dust
that blooms on a polished table,
fleet wild pollen.
Dusk's a wide, blue table
and we're numberless as the settling dust –
little souls, barbed like pollen
with selfish, unassuageable dreams.

Abroad at dawn, a ghost of water
carries with it rats'
yeasty leavings.

EVENING IN THE VILLAGE

after Béla Bartók

Something calls me,
repeatedly.

Distant music –
tintinnabulation of zinc bowls, *coo-ees* –

Like a cat called back at dusk
I move through high grass

towards that voice
as if it pushed me

as if it pulled me.

SONNET NINE – A COLESHILL CONCORDANCE

Fields, pale sky, ragwort crowding
a summer verge: these
have no value,
so what are they for?

Earth and sky, near and far
come streaming back each moment
to make examples of themselves:
we are the way we are.

The young cat pricks her ears.
Impossible to explain
the light that shines through their veined
silk. Is its tenderness her trick,

or the light's? Is it whim,
like dialogue in old skin-flicks?

A CHARM AGAINST KNIVES

The 22-year-old personal assistant went missing from the Suju nightclub in Swindon on 19 March. Her body was found near the Uffington White Horse in Oxfordshire last week.

— Press Association, 1 April 2011

She lies under the earth; that earth
lies under your skin
like a bruise,
or the way dirt

seems a quality
of skin itself —
in the shadow cast
by illness's pallor,

or when a tendon
tightens in your calf
and brushes the bike's
oily chain

as you tread hard uphill —
Arriving at last
you might forget the strain,
going in with the others,

and only when a friend
asks *What's that bruise?*
remember the whisper
of steel on skin.

How urgent it is,
this never being free
of soil beneath your skin,
of dirt on your skin.

AN OXFORDSHIRE ANNUNCIATION

So many ladybirds in Coleshill, and so many
colonising my house in this frost-pocket

under the hill. Stunned
by indoor heat, they drop onto windowsills,

bed-covers, floors and chairs;
little messengers blown off-course,

they flatten and open like paper hearts –

NIGHT MUSIC

Symptom

Some nights, my body wakes
to itself:

a forest of cries and small deaths
as bruised tissues

punish each other
in the intimate dark.

I wake too, falling
from an electric sky

streaked with the flight paths
of sleepers, and loud

with shrieks: comets,
or the angels making music in hell.

Wait

I'm afraid.
Walls stand at angles
to the day.

No-one answers
when I call.
The rooms are light-struck.

It's midsummer
or midwinter.
I wake alone

and see fear
like dirt
under the daylight –

fear not cancelled ever,
but shadow-struck
by happiness.

Diagnosis

A phone rings
and suddenly flocks of starling
are shuttling across the dark,

in the beginning
passes its conjuror's
hand over chaos . . .

A phone rings,
setting the night
in motion.

Lifting, dropping –
birds everywhere burring
the vertiginous sky.

SONNET TEN – THE LADDER

A ladder raised in Coleshill
leads into the summer sky.
An old longing
clambers up it, fierce as desire.

The village climbs the hill.
Everything is hoping and dreaming
and the eye
shifts higher, still higher.

Picture the village. Picture especially how
the horse chestnuts and the church tower
draw it tight, gesturing
at a blue sky dashed with cirrus –

Picture ghostly neighbours with us,
clustered round and squinting up.

HAWTHORN MILK

The hawthorn brings death into a house.

Thorn-lily runs beside the fields
to meet the sky

where the smell of rain-water and salt
is like an opening –

chalice or drain, the mouth soft
and wet

This smell is meat,
not hawthorn,

the animal that turns and turns nearby
is not the sea

*

You were a breast
where I drank rusty milk
that made me yours

The rust peeled from your hands
and stained my skin
like ochre, like blood

When you died
my skin turned black
When we danced the *macabre*

your skin turned white
as the flowers of a Northern spring,
and I was your milk hope

The taste of blood in milk
is like rust; the smell of death
is like hawthorn blossom

*

Hawthorn stars the sky,
black against daylight
Its odour
is close and creaturely at night

How is it drugs
can give the skin
this deathly perfume
of hawthorn?

Familiar dark head
crowned with bright hawthorn –
your fear
is so lightly, so darkly worn

SONNET ELEVEN – SEPARATION

Back, further back . . . The fields
and woods aren't separate
or separable. They fit as sepals
fit a flower – a field-daisy

say, or purple clover
scuttling crabwise through the grass,
or meadow-sweet, which Edward Thomas
took for yellow upland parsley.

All of these, conniving,
pass fullness to and fro
the way kids pass the ball –
playing in the dusk

out beyond the boundary
where the trees drink down the light.

JERUSALEM

I saw also at Coleshill the most complete farm-yard that I ever saw, and that I believe there is in all England, many and complete as English farm-yards are.

— William Cobbett, *Rural Rides*

White stone in sunlight
baffles the eye.
Here are the pale
enclosed yards,

the alleys
between blocky walls
where shadows jam
like dial hands.

The dreamers
are in their stone beds.
Their breath condensing
into limestone

they exhale
gorgeous palaces, tenements,
a Righteous City
on earth.

GERONTIUS IN SCHOOL LANE

falling through / The solid framework of created things
            – Cardinal Newman, *The Dream of Gerontius*

He loves this inflected view:
small fields
on rainy hillsides

and lights
low between hedges
in the burred dusk.

The small rain, shadow-branches,
those standing shadows
that could be cattle –

these murmur to him
All is disunity,
things pile up like waste,

but – look – everywhere
are selvage,
margin, grace.

DAVE AND HIS HOLY MOUNTAIN

      Drive up Hannington yards, past the cars
without wheels,
without doors, all extravagantly rusted –
You imagine fireweed

      but the scrap sprouts meadowsweet, and there are larks
ceaseless overhead,
and threadbare cats squalling and climbing
over the stacked cars.

      His voice, in the naming of parts,
is tolerant Wiltshire
and watching him
is like watching a surgeon

      to whom you might give over
some sick limb,
or a bandaged head. You trust
his expert touch:

      seeing with what gaffer's care
from beneath its chassis he gentles a spanner
into the works
of the jacked-up Landrover.

SONNET TWELVE – DEER AT MIDDLELEAZE

Rhediad wybren, lwydwen lawdr
                              – Dafydd ap Gwilym

The deer racing across a field
of the same taupe and tallow
they are – if they *are*,
because they could be tricks of the light –
must sense themselves being poured
and pouring through life.

                    We tremble,
feeling everything's in motion,
and that feeling goes to and fro
in the world that shivers round us –
World, too, is something poured
and endlessly pouring itself.

February shakes the fields,
trembles in each hazy willow.

THE SOLOIST

You're wrong – the violin's not veneer,
its back's pure maple; and the belly's pine
makes each new note clear as a first thought.

Beyond all the technique is a prayer
that, when I need to, I will act –
only a part of me feels free
to shape the words I lack.

Every day comes the desire
to elbow through to some bright place
louder than a concert hall,
where the self echoes entire –
the outer to the inner call.

GLISSANDO

Self-portrait with the deer at Middleleaze

Sometimes at dusk
I have this sense
of really existing.

At dusk, deer
break their flight with odd
leaps. Earth-coloured,
they look like the arable
running across itself.

What if soil were water, able to eddy
and race –
the fields shifting, adrift?

I imagine looking down
from the barn roof.
To watch myself
is to slide across myself,
like pushing past a stranger.

PSALM OF THE COLESHILL WASHING LINES

Everything runs together –
sharp smells of spring,
the unreasonable brightness
of the peg, the sheet, the line that tethers

the sheet between sky and mud –
as if the garden marked a pause
in that eternal return
whose looping trace is blood

hissing through the ventricles.
What gives you life's the thing that kills.
All you need's this play of surface –
all that you need. All you have.

SONG OF THE STEPCHILD

The village is as perfect
as a snow-globe

on a summer table, a glass bloom
that seems to catch the light

and make it liquid.
Shake it, till snow

lies on imaginary pavements,
on windowsills, and in the sepals

of glass flowers –
There I am at home, there I am

in the lane, there
I am in the classroom –

One day soon I'll break
the glass skin;

as spring rain-storms
shatter the morning.

SONNET THIRTEEN – *LIEBESLIED*

The willow dips its silvered twigs
as if to assent to this:
the oldest cradle in the world
made of two consciousnesses

that, stretching in the wind,
embrace and rock each other so
who rocks and who is rocked
is undivided . . . All I know

is, leaning in towards the trunk,
I smell the green odour of earth
as it shifts. And later

I hear your hare's heart beat
and know you're moved by moving me.
How lightly that gets done.

SUMMERTIME

*If I had to show Coleshill off to a Yankee, I would blindfold him all the
way to, and after I got him out of, the village, lest he should see the scarecrows
of paupers on the road.*

— William Cobbett, *Rural Rides*

Gloriana in her gilded chariot, sweet-
chestnut and diesel, completes an historic circuit

of her desmesnes, backyards, purlieus, and tenancies
there-to-from;

gaudy peregrinations
to the musick of Sting and Elton John.

In Middle English gardens bodged
with bunting

the sun stares hotly
from among the roses.

*

No more *sweeting.*
No more *lulla lullay.*

No more sleepless bedrooms
far down those corridors

in cheap hotels
where a single wall-sconce flickers

through the dim hours;
just this missed encounter,

                              dropped

like a loose connection,
though something – still flaps and flickers.

*

High above the Atlantic
a sullen front

has its grip on the weather: storms –
sun – random

as punishment. *What pantheon
did we offend?*

we ask knowing
and refusing the answer.

I think, my dear, this is the end.
This is the end of everything.

SONNET FOURTEEN – TREMOR

The metals of the pipes do not agree,
and iron is the sacrificial anode
is what the landlord's plumbing expert
said when he called today.

And here comes a host of small exchanges
as if from the electric world:
pulses, tremors of antimony,
tremors under your skin at night.

Something is adjusting, or
anyway changing, iron
pipes and copper pipes at war –
a high-pitched shiver thrills the plumbing.

The house, the whole world, is shaking.
If you're not dead you're doing alright.

CODA

Beyond lathe and joist
under beams that creak
in summer heat,
night waits —

shadow-forest —
The window's moonlit;
you scrape your nail
along the wall

Moth, rat, ghost
flicker and wake
in the papery dark